# Covenant (With)

# Covenant (With)

Poems
by
Susan Bucci Mockler

© 2022 Susan Bucci Mockler. All rights reserved.
This material may not be reproduced in any form, published,
reprinted, recorded, performed, broadcast,
rewritten or redistributed without
the explicit permission of Susan Bucci Mockler.
All such actions are strictly prohibited by law.

Cover design by Shay Culligan
Cover photo by Tom Mockler, *Pause at Four Mile Run, Arlington, Virginia*. See more of his work at flickr.com/photos/tommockler/.
Author photo by Abby Greenawalt. See more of her work at abby@abbygreenawalt.com.

ISBN: 978-1-63980-200-5

Kelsay Books
502 South 1040 East, A-119
American Fork, Utah 84003
Kelsaybooks.com

*For my parents, Carmon and Pauline Bush,
and for Mary, Kathy, and Dave, my siblings, my people*

# Acknowledgments

Grateful acknowledgment is made to the editors and staff of the following publications, who published versions of these poems:

*Beltway Poetry Quarterly:* "Black Schist," "Mathematics of a Storm Surge" (Pushcart Prize Nominee)
*Bourgeon:* "Dark Energy," "Augury," "*Descansos*"
*Crab Orchard Review:* "How to Survive"
*Delmarva Review:* "Black Crows"
*District Lit:* "A Body Without Weight"
*The Forgotten River (anthology):* "Ministry of the River"
*Gargoyle:* "Civil War Hospital, Fredericksburg, Virginia"
*Maryland Literary Review:* "Covenant"
*The Northern Virginia Review:* "Presence"
*Peachvelvet:* "Ventriloquist's Instruction Booklet," "Waking"
*Poet Lore:* "The Chapel Street School Fire"
*Postcards Poetry and Prose:* "Upstate," "Fountain Grass"
*Washington Writers' Publishing House Writes:* "Snowdrift"


I am also grateful to David Keplinger, Kyle Dargan, @poets, the Virginia Center for the Creative Arts, and my awesome community of fellow writers.

# Contents

(with) Wonder

| | |
|---|---|
| Covenant | 15 |
| The ravine | 16 |
| Fountain Grass | 18 |
| Easter Morning | 19 |
| Augury | 20 |
| Perspective | 21 |
| Listen | 22 |
| Upstate | 23 |
| Osage Oranges | 25 |
| Cows in Carrollton, Georgia | 26 |
| Irises | 27 |
| Red Poppies | 29 |
| The Wind | 30 |
| What Matisse Taught Me About Rock Climbing | 31 |
| parallax of the heart | 33 |
| Ministry of the River | 34 |
| Release | 35 |

(with) Erasure

| | |
|---|---|
| The Chapel Street School Fire | 39 |
| Mathematics of a Storm Surge | 40 |
| Snowdrift | 42 |
| He'd Rather Live in an Iron Lung | 43 |
| Black Schist | 45 |
| Negative Space | 46 |
| A Body Without Weight | 47 |
| Fat | 48 |
| Commencement | 49 |
| Standard Issue | 50 |
| Acreage | 51 |

| | |
|---|---|
| Dear *Moonlight Sonata* | 52 |
| Beehive | 53 |
| Erasure | 57 |
| Exchange | 58 |
| Badlands | 59 |
| The Act of Dying | 60 |
| Learning to Drive | 62 |
| Dark Energy | 64 |
| How to Survive | 65 |

(with) Presence

| | |
|---|---|
| Diurnal Diary | 69 |
| Ministry of Presence | 74 |
| Ash | 75 |
| Waking | 76 |
| Instead | 77 |
| *Descansos* | 78 |
| If the Boys Were Dead or Alive | 79 |
| Ventriloquist's Instruction Booklet | 80 |
| Naming | 81 |
| Robotham's Creek | 84 |
| Insomnia | 85 |
| Space and time | 86 |
| can love still be found down here? | 88 |
| Certainty | 90 |

*But the wind blows there.
I reckon the wind
Must care.*

From "Restrictive Covenants" by
Langston Hughes, 1949

(with) Wonder

# Covenant

The horses thought they were waiting for you
to bring them in from the pasture, in from damp

night air, where sweet alfalfa, oats, hay, would be,
where they always are—the horses' names etched

in wooden plaques over their stalls: *Comet, Midnight,
Scarlet,* black iron latches securing them in, safely—

but they were waiting for you to make them whole
again, ache of yesterday's memory—evolving from

mere shapes, nothing visible but their eyes, squinting
to see their way out of the dark to you, warm air

steaming from their nostrils, withers, hocks: trot,
then canter, like a drum coming out of the darkness—

weightless gallop, hooves suspended above ground,
offering of loyalty and service. But you've been waiting

too—for them to see you, to turn your mist into body—
witnesses to this fundamental bearing of your days.

# The ravine

hugs the far
edges of
our garden,

a steep slope
of land, shaped
by ice sheets—

advancing,
retreating:
giving, then

taking back,
leaving silt,
sediment,

rock; a place
nothing grows—
not milkweed,

wild carrots,
lamb's ears,
not cattails,

even in this
dampened soil.
What more

can I tell you
about this
ravine but

that it marks
edges, that it
resembles

mystery,
as how
we need

to mark
our end-
ings, our

leavings,
all our
own edges?

# Fountain Grass

Today, I am
soloist,
lone dancer

on a backlit stage.
I've been waiting
all night,

poised, my silver
feather plumes
curled forward,

resting.
Then sunrise,
my cue

to wake, to stretch
my slender waver-
ing stalks:

body must become
one—with mind,
with wind and rain

and breath,
with love—
the graceful

arch
in the small
of the back

# Easter Morning

I've seen ghosts who have bodies
and men and women who do not,
and I'd like to think the red fox I saw

in the yard Easter morning was real—
even knowing my eyes were still
filled with moonlight and dreaming.

The fox was just sitting there,
quivering in the breaking light,
ears pointed, alert, as if it'd heard a voice.

Its brown eyes stared right past me
to the forsythia about to burst open,
but before I could wake anyone,

it was gone—no flesh, no bones, no body,
nothing but the pewter-colored sky,
tinges of red in the grass.

# Augury

*after* Relative *by Sam Gilliam*

The sky washes over me, enticing,
bursting open with orange and teal,

a cleansing becoming more vibrant
from west to east. Soft, like a cotton

scarf I'd drape lightly over my shoulders
on a cool night, its ends fluttering—free,

unfettered. I can smell the storm coming.
Sweet, musky earth. Metal taste burns

my lips. Sediment. A change, inevitable.
For some, eruptions—colors bleeding

together, blot of black, subduction.
For others, swells of peach, turquoise,

lavender, a stroke of yellow, autumn rush,
perhaps. I enter the sky's conversation.

# Perspective

The path to Sparrow Pond
has become too familiar; I don't
notice birds unless they swoop
in front of me—and only robins,
cardinals, blue jays, occasionally
a goldfinch or hawk—lofting in
the wind. I have become stale
in my meditative walks: what once
had offered respite, new energy,
has become another item to be
checked off a list, only seeing
that which stands out, but knowing,
instinctively, I am missing out—
that it's time for something new.
And this day, I decide, the difference
will be not place, but perspective.
The Cooper Hawk will not be bird,
but weight, its body bearing down
upon this world in heaviness, upon
the dead cedar, the weight of him
watching, his glassy red eyes
trained on me—every movement
a question—asking what happened
to this body he's witnessing today,
what has made it seem so different?

## Listen

the path is scattered
        this October morning
        with black walnuts
        brownish-green husks

fleshy as fists tightened
        around brown-nut fruit
        a sign that time
        is clearing its throat

has been waiting
        its turn to step up
        to the podium
        its rusty voice

crackling
        the morning air
        forcing us
        to attention

to witness the sky
        darkening earlier
        and earlier
        each day

# Upstate

Mile after mile
of farms,
rolling hills,
dairy cows,
an apple orchard
in the backyard,
poison sumac
at the edge
of the garden
dripping red.
Mountains
and mountains,
lakes
and more lakes,
ice stretching
its long fingers,
pushing boulders,
dirt,
and sand
into end moraines.
Leatherstocking tales,
headless horsemen
galloping through our dreams,
old, bent Ichabod
hobbling off
in shame,
nine pins on Sunday
afternoons up on the highway.
Elderberries
and blackberries
glistening in the sun
along the ditch bank.
Cattails and milkweed—

their fine white
wisps of cotton
sticking to our hands
when we'd try
to blow them
away.

# Osage Oranges

I step into this September
as if my body is not attached,
into a space of goldenrod,
monarchs, and the confounding
contradiction
of the Osage orange—
its knobby tuberculated
outer shell more green
or yellow than orange,
inedible, resembling
contours of the brain.
I step as if my body
no longer remembers
distance traveled between
two points, latitude
or longitude, function
of cortex,
of touch, nor understands
the hippocampus
of memory,
but is aware
that I will lose you
one day—
that I will lose
history, language
and be destined
to learn to speak
without words.

# Cows in Carrollton, Georgia

*after James Wright*

As the fog lifts
in Carrollton, Georgia,
the great brown eyes
of the Holsteins soften.
They lift their heads
at the noise we make.
They've been sleeping
and grazing in the pasture,
but seem happy we stopped,
though they pretend they're not.
They are too proud,
or maybe too focused
on chewing.
Crusty tongues lap
slow licks of salt,
their bulging sides touch
and warm each other,
like coals igniting a fire,
We reach out to stroke their ears,
thinking that if these were horses,
we would ride them.
They are black and white.
Their tails switch back and forth,
sweeping at flies.
Suddenly, they see us—
our eyes meet,
the skin on their lips quivers,
having just stepped
through some veil—
that hung, like a curtain,
between us.

# Irises

*on the anniversary of my mother's death*


One day,
brown leaves
patches of snow,

then, as if
from nowhere,
the first shoots

burst out
of winter's
dusky coffin

blanketing the yard
in a rainbow
of color.

I cut purple
irises for you
today, place them

in a vase
on the mantle,
bundled

in delicate
lavender ribbon,
their sturdy

stalks propped
against each other
in the glass,

their sword-like
petals falling down,
opening.

# Red Poppies

Not seeing is the way. You can be transformed into something else: a speck of dust, perhaps, or a light ray, or air, as though you've left your body behind. You can become light, darkness, color, shadow, subject. You can become red poppies in a red vase. Layers upon layers of red. Screaming red. You can become the moment of emptiness in the gallery. A simple vase with four red flowers bursting loneliness. Anonymous. The moment light changes to dark, the moment you transform and can no longer see your reflection in the glass frame. Only color beneath color. Only what is left in your absence.

# The Wind

*after Robert Creeley*

All night it lashes
the glass, keeps me
from sleep.

Switching, slashing,
this screaming,
insistent wind.

Who am I
to this wind jousting
at my window?

This intruder, who
might want nothing
more from me

than a safe place,
a haven to rest
its brokenness?

What love have I
to offer any damp-
ened, tired soul?

This trusting wind,
trembling, lays down
next to me.

# What Matisse Taught Me About Rock Climbing

The body must be willing
to come apart,
to see itself

not as body, but as hand,
torso, spleen, individual
elements

gripping outcrop.
He culled the studio
for gouaches—

opaque watercolors—
brushing them
onto white paper, cutting

out gardens,
leaves, and fruit.
The body will think

it needs strength—
it will scour
the rock face, make

tentative grabs
toward the pink
and gray crystals.

But, it will need
to transform.
He'd pin the cut outs

to the wall, watching
them flutter in the breeze—
rearranging, until the papers

announced flower, bird,
angle that hair splays
at the nape

of a blue nude's neck.
There is no need to anchor
the rope. No need to belay.

The truth of the body
is genius; it knows
how to separate.

Ascent begins
when body becomes
whole again, revenant.

# parallax of the heart

let the heart work harder/
for you/take it out/and hold/
it in your hands/let it/do more/
than love/let it/be light/
your eyes straining to see/let it
embrace/rather than/
dismiss/darkness/
mirth/dying alone/let it
be/ancient redwoods
rooted/for ten lifetimes/
or more/let it/finally/
use rush of blood/last gurgle/
for more than love/let it/
gaze/at petals jellyfish symmetry/
pulse blue aura/of the moon/
ice crystals/let it/linger/

# Ministry of the River

Like ospreys, kingfishers,
double-crested cormorants
seeking out a sycamore, red

oak, or beech—I, too come
to the river seeking refuge,
a stop-over, hoping to stay

my persistent restlessness,
the river calling me again—
and again, her calm waters

glistening like rare diamonds
in the sun, her quiet rippling
an invitation to come closer—

*retreat*, she whispers, *rest
in my sanctuary—as I carry
silt, pebbles, sediment, I will*

*carry your troubles, too—
release all sadness, all grief
to my waters, watch them*

*float downriver, disappear—
breathe in my monarchs,
peepers, pale yellow irises,*

*breathe in my bullheads,
my striped bass, even my
rat snakes—breathe deeply,
breathe, daily benediction.*

# Release

When I hear
the urgent honking,
look up to see
their standard
v-formation,
I know it's time, too,
for my migration.
Not south,
seeking warmer days
and nights,
more hours
of direct sun,
but toward water.
Driven by instinct,
my body craves
its buoyancy,
force thrusting
against me,
keeping me afloat,
as though
I've left my body;
its mystery
of the unseen:
flat rocks polished smooth,
catfish circling,
venom ready,
sudden drop-offs,
trenches,
places to hide a body.
I wait for release
and ask only this:
do not look away.

(with) Erasure

# The Chapel Street School Fire

My mother worried that dead people would suck me out of her belly before I was born, like the myth that cats suck breath out of babies, killing them. She'd heard dead people miss their own babies, and you have to be careful they don't take yours. So, when the Chapel Street School burst into flames and my mother rushed down there looking for her younger sister, Margaret, who was only 8, she hid her bulging belly beneath my father's old trench coat so that the gray arms of the dead would not reach up out of the ground to try to snatch me from her. But what my mother didn't know was that I'd already wiggled out on my own and was sitting in a tree, watching. I saw flames whipping through the school, burn it to the ground. I saw children run out onto the blacktop, their breath hanging in white puffs in the frozen air. I heard their screams. Smoke burned my eyes. I saw frantic parents block the streets with their cars, small bodies lined up on the grass, eyes glued to the sky. Then I saw my mother walk home with her little sister, the trench coat wrapped tight around her.

# Mathematics of a Storm Surge

What we
can measure,
we think we understand:
ratio
of sand to sea,
height
of wave to base,
depth
of sediment.
At times, we are
a barrier island,
a narrow strip
of sand,
helpless,
in the seething sea.
What we
can count,
we think we can save:
bodies drowned,
houses demolished,
but not how the wind
heaves and groans,
how sand migrates
down the coast,
changing its shape
how layers of mud,
shells,
dead grasses
scatter
on flattened dunes—
a hazy salty air
lingering
over us,

the coast rambling,
without measure,
out to sea.

# Snowdrift

You could walk into my grandmother's kitchen
in winter and smell oranges—orange peels
she'd strewn on her stove top, the oven turned low,
warming the house, the scent filling it, reminding
her of the grove she'd left behind in the hills
of Le Marche, a place she thought would be home forever.
When her words faded and her eyes glazed, losing focus,
you could tell she was right back in the orange grove
in Ancona, 10- or 12-years-old, laughing, snaking
around the trees with her sisters, juice dripping
down their chins, staining the white blouses
they'd picked from the clothesline that morning.
She might have been trying to remember
where she'd buried the orange blossoms she'd carried
on the crossing—the ship rocking in the dark water,
her sisters and mother huddled close, then them all living
together in this house, before she was alone, sitting
on this stool by the stove watching snow pile high
on her windowsill, until she couldn't see
one more thing through the glass.

# He'd Rather Live in an Iron Lung

We knew to find him
        in his bike shop,
                patching
inner tubes,
air pumps hissing
           and throbbing
                in permanently greased hands.

But that was
        before sickness,
               gangrene,
black mummified sores
            on his skin—
                toes, then foot, then leg
        cut off.

We moved his bed
        to the front room,
             where he became furnishing—
a place to drop a coat.        Even we
        closed our eyes,
              turned
                away from the sagging,
                      rancid skin—
      remains of a body
           beneath stiff sheets.

He'd rather live in an iron lung,
        metal kingdom for one,
                Saint
            of all things metal—
hard, opaque,
        blocking

    all light and touch,

                    Saint
          of a world

of tubes and pumps    breathing for him,

          Saint
                    of a world he'd invent,

trading metal for wings.

# Black Schist

When I heard the doctor say he saw nothing
but membranes, I fell backward into someone else's body.
When I heard those words, I knew the place in me
where you had been had already begun turning to stone—
that sand and mud and water would compress
layer by layer over time, into a type of rock
that does not seem to erode, even as rain
and wind may scrape across my face.
I gather in your absence every day,
your tiny flakes of grain splitting so close
to the cast of what they could become.

# Negative Space

*Pompeii, A.D. 79*


Bending in their gardens pruning fig trees,
mulching vineyards, or simply fixing
bread and cheese for lunch.
The village disappears in white wind,
dust blackens the sky, as though the moon
stalled out in front of the Earth, blocking the sun.
Thirteen hollow spaces, blinded by layers of ash,
thirteen mouths filled with gravel and fire,
drowning the sounds of each calling to another.
Who will find them? Put names to these voids,
outlines of the shapes they'd been that morning,
mothers shielding children, hands touching only air,

# A Body Without Weight

The stairway
in my house
seems to narrow
with each step
I take upward,
until, at the top,
there is nowhere
left to go
but into the open arms
of a vanishing point,
into the open arms of a body
without weight.
I can't feel my hands
in this place.
I can't feel
any part of me.
I feel only other
vanishings I've known:
heavy white peonies
bent to the ground after a rain,
velvet stems
of my mother's gladiolas
growing by the door,
me, standing in a snowy field
of broken cornstalks,
my red jacket
buttoned to my chin.

# Fat

My mother and aunts
used to dig them out of the warm soil—
their hands closing around the bulbs,
as though they held a treasure.
I string them in garlands for decoration
in my kitchen, like white roses—
their translucent skin protecting me
from sickness and demons.
But, each time I chop or mince or scrape
the bulbs into hot oil, my dead mother and aunts
crowd in, peer over my shoulder,
making sure I get it right—
*Caponato, tacozze e fagiolini, baccala all'aquilana*
How they'd roar on Sunday afternoons—
random talk while playing pinochle:
this one uses too much garlic in her sauce,
this one not enough, how can she call that sauce?
What they say to me each day sounds different:
*Why did you leave? What did you hope you'd find
in a city white as ice, in a country fat with snow?*

# Commencement

*for G.N.*

Tall and sturdy as the bamboo shoots
rooting in her backyard, resilient, hurt-
ling toward the future at breakneck
speed, versed early in the language
of power: teachers who taught *can't,
less than*, not seeing past a quiet, dark-
skinned girl—a father who taught *absence,
good-bye,* that *this is how men are.*
A mother who taught *yes, please, stay,*
but the girl is already leaning away from home,
reaching out toward her own re-birthing,
who, despite her anxious body, shrieks
to the darkening sky each night:
*Just let them try to taste this blood of mine.*

# Standard Issue

I came for the jacket—
standard issue for troops,
designed for eminently
decent men.

Stashed in the back closet
with my mother's
worn, forgotten dresses,
I knew I'd need it one day.

I think of you at the front—
this light-weight cropped
waist offering little warmth.
It's always snowing

in my memory of you.
Though you may think
I need the jacket to keep you
close, I wear it for the letting go.

# Acreage

I find my way down
what once was a well-worn path—
covered now with burdock
and jewelweed, burrs clinging
to my clothes and hair.
The walls of the milk house
are moist and crumbling,
the chicken-coop door hangs
by one hinge, strands of hay
and hardened droppings litter
its floor. The shed's windows
are broken, paper wasp nests
drape its doorways, their message
clear: *you don't want to come
in,* yet I do. I want to stand
in its brokenness—of tractor
tires and onion crates, corn
planters, and tar paper,
to embrace the wasp stings
on my arms and legs, feel
the red welts rising. I stand
at the edge, imagine a freshly
plowed field, my father bent
in planting, the seedlings
dwarfed in his massive hands.

# Dear *Moonlight Sonata*

The pianist believes he can understand life
by playing your dark chords of lamentation,
your joyful chords, like spectral wind rustling
through wildflowers before a summer storm.

He knows full well there is conversation to be found
somewhere between your darkness and your light,
but it is a language he cannot speak on his tongue—
until he strikes C-sharp minor, D-flat minor,

*be it, be it,* you say to him, *sostenuto, allegro,
vivace,* this language he knows, and he is no longer
the man he was when he woke, but he becomes
those chords and nothing more, brought to a place

halfway between being and not being, a place
he can cry tears he needs to cry, or scream,
or laugh, or love with such fierce accuracy
that when he sees his hands moving over the keys,

he thinks, *these are not even my own.*

# Beehive

1.

   The honeybee's hexagon hive   is the perfect shape

      for a home—a six-sided structure

      built to raise their young—

   tiling off equally-sized

         partitions,

  minimizing

        each cell's

perimeter,

     reducing

     the time needed for building,

   leaving more

     for dancing the tail waggle

     and buzzing—

  shaking their abdomens,

       spiraling, zigzagging,

striking each other
                    to communicate
         nearby food or danger.

2.

*Beehive,* the unofficial name for rows of tenement
housing littering the banks of the green, murky
Erie Canal, tenements my ancestors called home,
my ancestors who came here to work the muck—
rich, black soil primed for onions and potatoes,
my ancestors who came poor and without papers,
who didn't ask for this life of grime, crowded,
roach-infested, broken windows, no heat, no
landlord willing to fix its brokenness or trap
the rats that oozed their way out of the muddied
canal waters, scrambling for fallen crumbs, my
ancestors who first crossed the ocean to Arkansas,
becoming sharecroppers on plantations before migrating
North, who had picked cotton, whose fingers had bled
and skin shred from the sharp cotton bolls, promised
they'd own their own land when they picked one acre,
when they picked two acres, when they picked three,
when they picked a thousand, when they picked acre
after acre in their sleep, when they realized no acres
would ever exist for them, not ever in this nightmare.

3.

As far as anyone knows, bees can't swim.
They are, however, attracted to swimming
pools, foraging the placid surfaces for bugs.
This, I learned too late, and inconveniently—
scooping what I thought to be a dead bee
from our pool turned out not to be a dead
one, but a fierce stinger, puffing and bloating
my hand, searing my skin a deep crimson red,
delaying my family's trip to the amusement
park—my family, waiting in the car, once
again showing distressing immunity to pain.

# Erasure

I imagine he is my son. He doesn't have eyes. No ocular tissue. No opaque film that might let in even one speck of light or movement or shadow. Just skin where his eyes should be. His disease only occurs when a mother and fetus both carry a *RBP4* mutation. People will blame the mother—

it's always the mother's fault. In my family, we might purposely pronounce the word wrong: *An-o-phth-al-mia.* If he, his older brother, and I would be eating burritos in a fast-food restaurant, people might stare, then quickly look away. His brother and I would pay no attention to the mess he would make or to these people. They might be ashamed if I caught them staring, likely happy he isn't their child. Sometimes their looks might be sympathy. I would pretend I didn't see them. The blind have developed the ability

to locate obstacles by making clicking sounds. For weeks after looking at the sun during the total eclipse last summer, I was afraid I'd go blind. My son's hands would wave around in the air, helplessly trying to locate his mouth. Like echolocation used by bats or swiftlets, or shrews, but he wouldn't yet be able to make the high-pitched sounds or hear their echo. His face and his arms would be covered in salsa and pieces of burrito. I would always bring a wet washcloth with me. I would wipe him clean.

# Exchange

I am slipping a dirty tee-shirt,
a pony with a pink flowing mane on its front,
over my 10-year old's head,
helping her try on her first bra.
A melon-colored padded size 32 double A,
a traditional white front-clasp,
a stretchy, sporty navy thing.
She loves them all.
My daughter stands before me—
dirty and sweaty from the first warm spring days
of baseball and soccer in the street
with her brothers.
She's so proud of her winter sprouting,
unlike me, who tried to deny my own
and that anything would ever be different
from what it once had been.
My daughter is ready to jump in
and not look back—and somehow knows to call
upon my mother in this fitting room
in a discount department store in the suburbs—
hoping a dead woman she's never met
can intervene where I cannot and be with her
as she begins to become this changeling,
this girl, changing right in front of me.

# Badlands

deposition: tiny grains of sediments,
sand, silt, and clay cemented together.
fire roars through ancient riverbeds.
a dragonfly has no place to land.

a three-toed horse grazes on gumweed.
alligators lurk in muddied rivers.
it's always daytime here.

light-colored ash covers our bodies:
fantastic shapes rise from floodplain.
black mud on the seafloor hardens
into shale; the sea drains away.

erosion: an ordinary looking woman
dressed for church leans over a railing
and shakes the dust from her front-
porch welcome mat; she will disappear.

# The Act of Dying

*for Laura Bhadra*

1. Act

The act of dying is a formal affair.
You'll want to look your best.

Get your hair styled, a manicure,
a new dress. Slough off layers of dead

skin, slather on whipped-ginger lotion.
When you're ready, carry in your gifts:

banana yogurt, a peace lily, asters.
Her hands and legs will be twitching,

morphine will continuously be dripping.
She may think you're her dead sister;

she may call you Jean. When the doctor
says the words, *quality of life, hospice,*

fall to the floor. Hit your head on the edge
of the table, bleed. Relish these moments

of unconsciousness. Nurses will wheel you out
for stitches and x-rays, a tetanus shot, even.

You'll be the one who will leave this room,
but neither of you will eventually heal.

2. Black Crows

We could never be them,
cawing out our omens of death,
making our presence known outside her window.
No, we hovered round her bed like hawks,
at times gliding, as though weightless,
waiting for a rising wind current
to catch us and hold us aloft,
keeping safe distance between our bodies and hers.
But, there were no miracles left in this room—
not transfer of heart to soul to wing of feathery dust,
not ascendant hymns of praise or longing or fear,
no body made pure and whole and strong again.
Only us, in a final dive down to her, anticipating,
stretching our wings back past our heads.

## Learning to Drive

It is not a horse, my father said,

the first time I sat behind the wheel

of our Fairlane 500, a monster of a car,

a V-6 engine, built for drag racing,

I learned later. You are in control here,

he said, not like Max, his old blonde

Belgian chewing alfalfa in the pasture

behind the barn, who had known

by instinct, it seemed, to pull the plow

in a straight line, digging a furrow,

all the while keeping steady pace,

my father needing only to voice

a clear command—*gee, haw, whoa,*

back, or tug the rein a slight left or right.

Max knew, too, his reward at day's end—

his heavy, leather collar lifted, releasing,

my father brushing sweat and dirt

off his coat until it shone, the water

bucket filled, the hay rack brimming,

freedom to gallop across the field.

# Dark Energy

*after Sandy Hook*


Notice what you remember this day:
how clean the air smells,
how warm it is for winter,
how you hoped it would be snowing.
Notice how bare the trees are,
black birds perched
in the empty branches,
cracked ice on a puddle.
Notice lips, hair, skin,
fingertips, tongue,
the place in the sky
you saw the first star
last night and closed your eyes,
from habit, wishing, wishing, wishing.

Notice what you won't remember:
how quiet it was the moment
after the gunshots,
that the screaming
sounded like coyotes in the desert.
Notice blur of smoke,
river of blood,
skin stuck to walls, missing faces.
Notice your question:
why must a coffin
hold a child,
why not rocks, mud,
burnt wind, even water?
Notice there is no waking from this dream,
the sky will always be this dark.
the only living will be living
on the edge of a black hole.
Notice a million stars exploding daily.

# How to Survive

Do your homework. Each kind of airstrike—shells, rockets, phosphorous bombs, cluster bombs—makes its own unique sound. Why wouldn't it? High-pitched squeaking, clicking, rumbling, like thunder, even buzzing. Learn the differences. Learn, by their sound, how close they are to you. How much time you'll have to take cover. There is always one you won't hear. There's no use worrying about that one. Live on the lower floors of buildings. Stay out of the rooms near the streets. We use ours for storage. You won't have to worry about lights attracting bombers or snipers. There won't be any electricity. It's almost always dark. Smoke. Smoldering rubble. It's best to spend most of your time inside. You'll be bored, but you have to believe life will be normal again. One day. If you have a car, use it sparingly. Hide it in an empty garage or shop. Make sure to keep the car windows cracked just a bit. Otherwise, the glass may shatter from the pressure of bombs exploding nearby. That happened to me. Not twenty feet behind me. I never heard it coming. The windshield shattered. When you kiss your wife or run into your friends on the street, look them in the eyes. Look deeply at them. Memorize every inch of them. Tell them you love them. Tell them again. It may be the last time. Tell them how happy you are that you are together. Stay calm. Above all, you have to stay calm. Remember why you choose to stay. It is your city. It is your country. You must absolutely insist on it.

*Inspired by "We Live in Aleppo. Here's How We Survive," by Omair Shaaban, The Washington Post, Oct. 23, 2016.*

(with) Presence

# Diurnal Diary

1. Morning

Silence, but for the banjo-
.....like twanging
..........of bullfrogs
in the swamp, hidden
.....in the reedy
..........cattail stalks,
.....froglets leaping out
of the water, a swift splash,
..........gasping
for air, learning to breathe,
.....and me, wanting
to stay,
.....immobilized,
..........wanting
.....to memorize
..........their movements,
.....so terrifyingly simple,
so undeniably magnificent.

2. Mid-Day

Conceding to the work
that must be done—
sitting at a desk,
practicing addition
or subtraction
on a whiteboard,
chopping onions
and potatoes
for a dinner stew
rather than out
walking the dog,
shooting free throws
on the basketball court,
even weeding
the tomato and flower beds.
Maybe later,
maybe tomorrow,
but, right now
no motion,
nothing
detected
but the rustling
of Aspen leaves
in a faint mid-day
breeze.

3. Twilight

Sun disappears
      over the horizon—
      one moment shining,
           the next, vanished,
      as though the large round orb
                dropped suddenly
          into the sea.
Sky's remaining light
      diffuses into pink—
          sacred time,
              a time for dreaming,
                  suspended
         between
      no longer day
             and not yet night,
      suspended
          between
still here
              and not yet gone,
    suspended,
        grieving
what we left
              undone,
    unseen,        unspoken,
          unfinished,
                grieving
      possibilities.
Cyclical eventide,
          catapults us forward
as each star lights the darkness        around us,

until
        the last
                of many stars
        appears.

4. Dusk

I expected to hear
someone
walking through
the night with me—
a voice, at least,
or footsteps shuffling
along the path.
I cannot be the only one
who needs this darkness
to be fully visible,
this solitude of time
to realize its speed.
No distractions
but the beating
of my own heart,
my own breath
rhythmic, pulsating
in this darker stage
of twilight—
a sliver of the moon
lingering,
offering—
me, refusing
again.

# Ministry of Presence

The woman slept:
her head flopped off
to one side, her mouth
rounded into a perfect *O*,
like mouths of choir boys
in animated film.
I stood by the side
of her bed, not sure
how close to come
and rubbed my new brass pyx.
It held three wafers
I'd taken from the tabernacle
that morning.
How peaceful a room,
I thought. I'd want this:
a window opening onto a garden,
hum of traffic and ceiling fan,
a vase of fresh blue flowers
on the windowsill.
They could be asters or bluebells.
It wouldn't matter.
I read the cards
from her family. Would anyone
save them, layered
between tissue paper
and lavender?
The woman slept.
I was nothing to her
in this room.
In my car,
I ate the three wafers.

# Ash

Today, I need to climb
this tree—not the sycamore
of Jericho—but a 60-year-
old ash in my front yard,
its branches still covered
in ice and snow. Slipping,
sliding. I grasp toward
fissured bark for finger
and toe holds. I need
this tree's height for lift,
like the blue jays darting
around my head, bold
and fearless, chattering
their complaints. I need
vantage—to lift me
past this view, these dreary
days. I need to witness
a place of new suns shining,
of kinder worlds, a view
from which I can descend
the same way I rose—branch
by branch, one trembling
leg then the other.

# Waking

In the middle of the night
in a chair in the living room,
having fallen asleep
reading again, the lights
still burning, my book having slid
from my lap to the floor,
then waking, confused,
until I remember—
the rooms—all those rooms
scattering my dreams—bedrooms,
living rooms, cellars, stairways,
some imagined, some real—
all darkened, and I understood
that I'd been building, at night,
a house that needed to exist
in darkness, without knowing why
that mattered or without knowing
that darkness is a myth, appearing
only as a lessening of light,
not a thing unto itself,
and that in these dreams,
scattering the dark
is the way I understood building
my house,
photon chasing photon,
subtraction.

# Instead

*for Father Frank Desiderio*

The priest didn't know
what to say,
so, he spoke,

instead, of how his father
taught himself
the accordion

and that the crippled fingers
could squeeze out
the right notes

to the *tarantella*
until the end,
and, he spoke, instead,

of how his father
loved to play
on Sunday afternoons

under the maple
by the river
because the leaves

seemed to listen
as they floated
downstream, counting.

## *Descansos*

I pass the time counting
mile markers. US89, Big Sky,
Painted Desert to Zion:
three-hundred-twelve,
two-hundred-forty,
then white crosses
draped with plastic
flowers
appear
in the grass
along the highway.

Each cross
someone's child.
I hold my breath.
A body remains
at rest unless that body
is in motion. The world
falls farther away
each day. Someone's child
ejected, roaring
lifeless
through this Navajo land,
sediment of manganese
and iron; their blood
and hair and skin
leach into the
ground, claiming
these spots
as their own.

# If the Boys Were Dead or Alive

This morning I couldn't help
thinking what it'd been like
for her during the war. She'd
talk about her brothers, fear-
ing they'd both died, saying,
*You kids didn't know what it
was like, not knowing from
day to day if the boys were
dead or alive.* That is the fear
she'd passed down to me, kill-
ing them both off in her mind,
hoping to prevent one brother's
plane from being shot down
or the other tripping a wire
in a field somewhere in Germany
or France, their bodies splinter-
ing apart into pieces she'd never
see again. It's like that now,
I thought, the unknowing.
All we do know to do is sit
in our living rooms reading,
listening to the fire crackling,
hoping that will be enough.

# Ventriloquist's Instruction Booklet

When you pull the string dangling
from the back of his neck, you will

be the one talking—make a *d* sound
for *b*, an *n* for an *m*, & *th* for *v*—no one

will notice the difference, and your lips
will barely move. The problem is Step 5:

*Convince yourself your partner's completely
alive.* Look him in the eye as he tells you

what he does all day—opens your closets,
tries on your blue blazer, your loafers, reads

your mail, pockets loose change dug out
of your sofa, even eats your leftover Thai.

You will have no choice but to believe
there is life in him, but, where is life

in you? Bring him to family gatherings.
When they begin chattering about him,

tell them how well he understands you,
tell them how our illusions never come easily.

# Naming

1. After *Three Young Buglers,* a photo

       These three,
barely old enough
            to hold themselves
   upright
            could be your children—
you'd tuck them in each night
          beneath heavy horse blankets
               kept folded at the end of their beds,
sure they'll still be breathing
      in the morning,
              small chests rising
        and falling
    in syncopated revelry.
        They've been born
   to fight,
imagining
        these bugles
  as muskets,
     balls spraying
          out of muzzles,
black powder
    covering their hands,
       rather than simply calling
   troops to formation,
           cold metal sticking to their lips.

2. Letter Written in Black Ink on the Baseboard of the Stone House

   *from Charles E. Brehm*

By all accounts, I am a handsome man—
six-foot-one, brown hair, hazel eyes, fair
complexion. Twenty-one, green but sturdy.
I am ready. Most days, I'm not afraid to die.
Give me my rations—pint of coffee, pound
of cornmeal, hard biscuits, vinegar. Please.

I marched to Manassas. Stood my ground.
I took a gunshot to my right leg—the ball
entered the inner and exited the outer thigh.
So. Much. Blood. Praise God the field surgeon
did not amputate. I wonder if he should have.
Whiskey became the medicine for my pain.

I crawled to the spring under the large oak
on the turnpike. I thought I might die there.
They took me prisoner and led me to a small
upstairs room, let me rest on a cot without a
mattress. I lost track of time, dreamed I heard
my mother building a fire. She was whistling.

I see severed legs heaped beneath that oak.
I beg someone, anyone remove them. I hear
groans of the dying all night. Horrid smells
of rotting flesh fill the air. So hot. This pen
feels smooth and cool in my hand. I curl my
fingers around it. I hold on tight. Black ink
drips to the wooden floor. I am not afraid.

                                        I write my name.

3. Cathedral of the Battlefield

I walk these grounds
as I would enter
a cathedral—quiet,
awed, aware. This
is sacred space. I
sense many of you
still here, hovering
through windstorm
and snow and sun,
names forgotten,
your precious scars
long ago healed,
searching
for your way
home. This cathedral
is not finished:
like a crumbling corner-
stone, rough-hewn
granite, tall towers
leaning, this place
need refurbishing.
This cathedral needs
prayers and candles
to light its darkness,
needs a different ending—
where all names
are remembered, where
all bodies
return home,
still breathing,
whole.

# Robotham's Creek

We went swimming in the creek
each summer, the same creek
the cows stumbled into, their
lumbering dappled bodies seek-
ing relief from the heat, their
cloven hoofs grappling the mud,
ignoring our cannonballs, our
shrieks as we slid down the em-
bankment, bloodsuckers latch-
ing onto our skin. We'd pull
the leeches off each other gently,
the final gesture before returning
home, hungry, like calves needing
a mother's milk, hungry for some-
one to say they know who we be-
long to, who our mothers are, that
the way home is always the way;
that it's always that simple.

# Insomnia

The smell wakes her at night—a sickening,
smoky meat smell. Ribs braising, pork

sautéing at 2:30 A.M. *Who does this?,*
she thought, cooks a full meal at this time?

Why aren't they asleep? The odors waft up
through the apartment's vents, sticking

in her throat. She'll have to open a window—
the one facing 22nd Street and entry ramp

to Rock Creek Park—where that girl was
murdered. What was her name? So many

girls killed in parks. Beths, Annas, Chandras,
daughters taken, leaving mothers lying sleepless,

remembering their sweet faces, voices, lavender
smells; mothers awake, cooking for their girls.

## Space and time

are not absolutes
but this life is;
the absolutes
of sunrise,
clouds, and rain,
of love, joy, grief.
I know it
each time
I step outside
feel a breeze
on my face;
gravity is not
simply a force
acting on an object
or mass;
it is the
force that propelled me
toward you, toward
living, the force
that propels me
still, toward home,
though the house
itself has long
been sold,
I keep
returning
if only for a few
moments—
to breathe in
the smell
of freshly plowed
dirt, hear
the basketball
bouncing
off the garage,

vibrating the metal rim,
to wonder, what else
has curved
around us while we
were looking elsewhere,
forcing us now
to bend
both forward and backward,
without place.

## can love still be found down here?

fading out
of space's vacuum
this is where our
dreams live:

a sliver, a flash,
enough to remember
auroras
shooting atoms

a solar wind
waterfall light
shivering sprite
meteorite

hopeful waking
airglow
ozone radiation
absorbed from the Sun

holes trap us;
hail, ice pellets
ice-clumped ribbons
dark memory

gasping
fragile ledges
granite mountains
blocking our path

bridge of prophets
river of blood
flowing garnet
seismic kisses

my heart's broken
doesn't know to cry
or fuse metals—
iron onto
nickel, spinning

# Certainty

We knew for certain this:
           my father's brother
was a horse thief. He skated
                across the St. Lawrence River.
        It shone like glass.
It's not certain
     if he ever arrived in Canada.

He carried only a loaf of stale bread

       and a photo of the horse.

            Refined, intelligent. A black
     Morgan.
Broad forehead, well-defined withers,
       muscular
hindquarters. She was said to win every race.

        He bent low on the ice,     knees 90-degrees
                           to the ground
    shifting body weight
from side to side:
      Chill of loneliness at his back.

          Fall, pause, glide—
for a second, suspended,   both feet off the ice:
    three-beat canter,

        four-beat gait,
                a horse in full
gallop.

# Notes

"Augury" was written during a virtual studio by Tara Campbell offered through the National Gallery of Art in Washington, D.C.

"parallax of the heart" has been put to music by Caroline Park and can be heard at https://youtu.be/fn4yPGndoxw.

*Descansos* translates as "resting place" and commonly refers to the crosses erected at the site of a violent, unexpected death. Some consider the last spot the body touches before death to be sacred.

The three poems under the title "Naming" were written during my time at the Manassas National Battlefield Park in Manassas, Virginia, as Writer in Residence.

The phrase "scattering the dark" is taken from the title, *Scattering the Dark: An Anthology of Polish Women Poets,* edited by Karen Kovacik.

# About the Author

Susan Bucci Mockler's poetry has appeared in numerous literary journals, including the *Maryland Literary Review, peachvelvet, Maximum Tilt, Pilgrimage Press, Crab Orchard Review, Poet Lore, The Northern Virginia Review, Gargoyle, The Delmarva Review, The Beltway Poetry Quarterly, The Cortland Review, The Paterson Literary Review, Lunch Ticket, Voices in Italian Americana,* and several anthologies. She leads poetry workshops on the segregationist history of Arlington County and teaches writing at Howard University. She lives in Arlington, Virginia with her family.

www.ingramcontent.com/pod-product-compliance
Lightning Source LLC
Chambersburg PA
CBHW030909170426
43193CB00009BA/789